I0817211

Tarot Goblinko

by Sean Ääberg

GOBLINKO

For the Love of God!

Tarot Goblinko: Dark Fantasy Medieval Punk Tarot

Photos by Katie Aaberg
Additional coloring by April Dimmick
Special thanks to the Kickstarter backers

For information about this title or to order other cool stuff, contact the publisher:

GOBLINKO
P.O. Box 90296
Portland, OR 97290 USA

www.goblinko.com

ISBN: 9781648411953

Printed in China

"The tarot is sacred." -Alejandro Jodorowsky

I love the tarot. I love that it is a symbolic system that you can use to try & understand life. I love that the more you bring to it, the more it gives back. I love that each card has an upright & reversed meaning which explores the positive & negative elements of these concepts. The tarot can be just a game or an occult divination tool or a tool for exploring the psyche, or all three. I love it on a hoky level, with its associations with fortune-telling & the like. I've tried to draw the tarot a bunch of times & have been blocked in different ways each time. The first couple of times I was blocked by being bored with the style I was working in & just having to tackle so many cards! 78 cards is no joke. Anyhow, in 2017 I realized that I could just keep drawing in the same style as long as I wanted having just finished Dungeon Degenerates:Hand of Doom & so I began the Tarot Goblinko. Katie would pick a card & I'd research it in our library & online & then draw it. The finished pieces were initially used for PORK covers, but eventually they started stacking up so quickly that they didn't get published. I completed 32 cards & then the hand of God struck me down & I had the stroke! The stroke wiped all my muscle memory & partially paralysed my left side making me have to relearn to draw with my non-dominant right hand. Because of these factors I can tell there is no way that I'm going to regain my old drawing style & that I've had to essentially relearn how to draw on the physical level, but not on the mental level. Because of this the Tarot Goblinko will never be completed as a card deck in the way I initially intended, but will exist in this book form, incomplete. Enjoy.

xox Sean Äaberg
Portland, Oregon.
Summer 2021

Other Attempts

I decided to draw a few tarot decks previous to my attempt at drawing the Tarot Goblinko. The first one used a lot of ideas that would eventually find their way into Dungeon Degenerates. I loved the way that drawing the tarot made my brain just expand on a subject & really think about the drawing in a way that was different from my approach before. Having all of these clear modes or systems for each drawing has been incredibly beneficial for me in terms of advancing my conceptual work. I also love it in terms of being a set of rules I could follow or break if I wanted. This is one of my obsessions. I basically forced myself to take the ideas I already had for drawings into this format that both confined & expanded them simultaneously like when you train a plant. Wonderful!

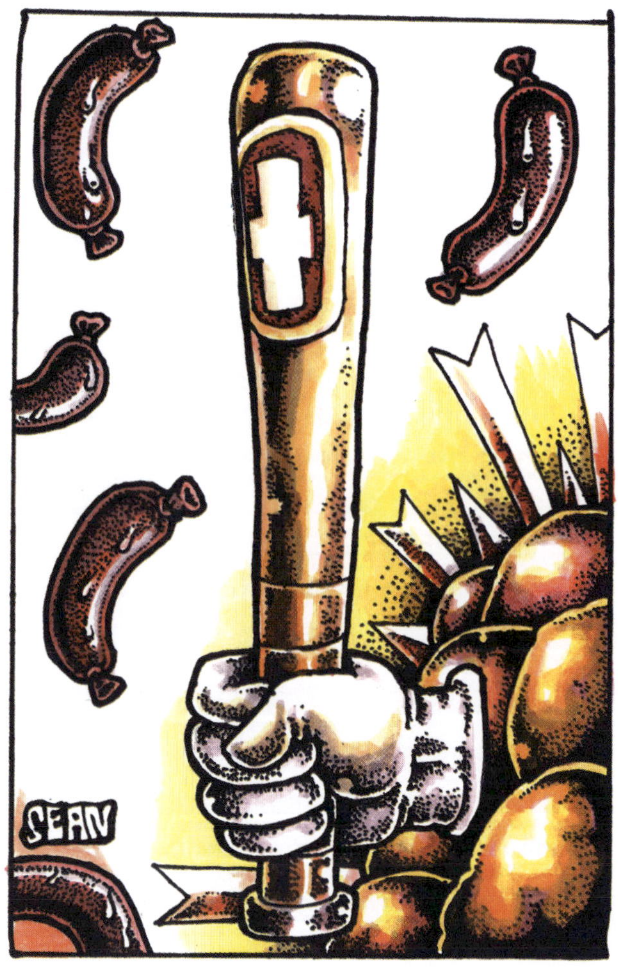

Wands

Part of my life work is sausages. I had this connection between sausages, police batons & the tarot suit of wands. Wands correspond to the clubs in ordinary playing cards. Wands are basically the penis, symbolically. The Wand stands for energy & willpower & that Yang spirit. The suit of Wands often represent a person's creative potential & can suggest themes of creative projects, inspiration & one's drive. The suit of wands also stands for the element of fire. I watercolored these cards in yellow, orange & red after John Blanche's "baked beans" color scheme. I like the sausage & the police baton for the same reason. I used to be a vegan & an anarchist, & I still have those leanings. But, through my own growth & my understanding of the complexity of the world & my desire to embody that complexity, I now enjoy the perversity of these objects & the negative & positive they can represent.

Tarot Rism

King Khan (aka Arish Ahmad Khan) did a tarot column for PORK called Tarot Rism where he would read the cards for various people (I'm remembering Greg Ashley & Nobunny) in his own eccentric, Rock&Roll method. I became friends with Arish through the magazine & eventually found out his intense love & respect for the tarot & that he had the tarot torch passed to him by Alejandro Jodorowsky. Arish asked me to draw his Black Power Tarot Deck in 2014 or so. While I was honored, I declined, stating that I thought a Black person should draw the deck. Eventually Arish got the artist Michael Eaton from Belfast to produce the images for the deck, as based on the Tarot Marseille which Jodorowsky looked over & eventually approved. I did draw King Khan as the Devil card for the Tarot Rism column!

XVI. THE TOWER

Heta Uma

I got obsessed with the Japanese Heta Uma style in 2008 or so. Heta Uma means "Bad but Good" & came into being in the 70s as championed by Garo magazine & popularized in the states by Gary Panter in the 80s. Part of what Punk taught me was that polish didn't matter, it was all about energy & spirit. The old three chord mythos. Heta Uma was liberating for me because at that time I needed permission to not care so much about the drawing. So, I started churning these drawings out & I eventually decided that I was ready to tackle the tarot. I got through more cards in this attempt than the first go, but still didn't complete the deck. I combined my Heta Uma style with this New York in the 70s flavor which I'm still digging upon looking at it.

VIII. JUSTICE

XI. STRENGTH

XV. THE DEVIL

XVIII. THE MOON

Lotería

I decided to do my own versions of the Lotería (Mexican Bingo) cards while doing the Heta Uma tarot. I didn't draw that many of them, but they were cool. I was just really into cards as an artistic medium.

42.

SEAN

LA CALAVERA

Tarot Goblinko

I started the Tarot Goblinko after I was pretty sure I could complete it. I was working on the longest lasting project me & Katie had ever worked on: PORK magazine & I'd just finished profusely illustrating DUNGEON DEGENERATES:HAND OF DOOM. While I was busy working on the deck & basically drawing contentedly every day I had the stroke. There's the old saying, "We plan, God laughs." The stroke knocked out all of my muscle memory & almost paralyzed the left, dominant side of my body forcing me to draw with my right hand. Luckily drawing is just one of the things I do. As I'm looking at it now, there is no way I'm going to draw like I used to again. My brain still works fine, I can write just like I used to (just slower) & I can pursue projects like I used to. Now I just work slower, have to rest & can't apply the DIY methodology to everything I do, just because I can't & everything is more difficult for me. Honestly I haven't been doing everything myself since me & Katie hooked up & even less since having employees. Writing about it feels more tragic than it does daily, where I just feel like I have to deal with the cards I've been dealt. I think that's the ultimate lesson here & it fits in perfectly with the Tarot Goblinko. You've got to deal with the cards you've been dealt.

The Major Arcana

"The true Tarot is symbolism; it speaks no other language & offers no other signs." - A. E. Waite

I came to the Tarot initially being more interested in the Major Arcana & its visual icons, but came to like the Minor Arcana equally the more I got into it. I dig the strong imagery found in the names of the cards & it is a world I prefer to pull from as the Minor Arcana deals with more specific, smaller issues. The Major Arcana started as being simple allegories but then gained occult significance during the occult boom of the 1700s. I like the cards being understood using both methodologies & don't really see a reason to keep the two separate. I like the limited scope of the earlier Tarot interpretations but we are where we are (where everyone is an expert & everyone has an opinion.) There are endless ways of looking at the cards & like art in general, the interpretation is up to the audience, despite that I have written a bit about each card & there is seemingly endless interpretation. If the art displays a number, this is the card's number. I made it through most of the Major Arcana thankfully but there are some significant gaps.

The Early Bird

"The early bird gets the worm."

I did this non-traditional card for people who supported the Kickstarter early. The older I get, the more these tired old aphorisms that didn't mean much to me as a kid seem progressively deep in a way that's very difficult to explain. Combined with my sudden interest in birds, it makes me feel old, like prunes old. The Tarot is not unlike these old aphorisms to me, they can be corny if they're said by a shallow person but can be totally deep if they are understood by a deep person. It all depends on your perception of the thing & what you bring to it. I guess that's like life. The Early Bird is shackled by its desire & its fear of missing out. The worms depicted are larval demons that the Early Bird eats. These larvae could turn into any kid of daemonic form if they feed off the right energy, in this case they are being eaten before they gain any power. The whole scenario takes place on some extra-dimensional plane with the Sun rising (it's early) & the Moon watching.

SEAN

The Fool

"Never tell a fool that he is a fool. All you'll have is an angry fool." - the Talmud

It is appropriate that the Major Arcana starts with the Fool, because you do indeed go through life as a fool until you accumulate enough wisdom to not be a fool. Dabbling in the Tarot can be a fool's errand. It's foolish to think that you don't start as a fool, the thing is, most people don't even start! Raising three kids, I've come to be overly familiar with the idea that the young & inexperienced don't want to be foolish, but they are. You just have a certain amount of time & reflection to put in, there isn't a way around it. For my interpretation of the Fool I used Japan's character Hyottoko as the base, mixed with a crusty traveller Punk. Hyottoko is a clownish character. In some parts of Japan, Hyottoko is regarded as the god of fire, in others he is just a comical personality. A Japanese folk tale tells that there was a boy with a bizarre face who could create gold out of his belly button, so when someone died in a house, you would put the mask of this boy at the top of the fireplace to bring good fortune to the house. I remember that a photo of a collection of Hyottoko masks in some book were listed as "masks of idiots" which I thought was humorously poetic & made a lasting impression on me. The dog is based on my own "Dee Dee", named for Dee Dee Ramone. She is also a fool. The Fool is nonchalantly walking along to the edge of a cliff he will probably fall off of, despite the warnings of his dog. The Moon & the Sun are both in the sky, & the Fool is more likely to be paying attention to them than he is to where he is going. There is a rotted out skyscraper consumed by the ocean, showing the inevitability of entropy of man's creations. The Fool carries a rose because he is a romantic.

SEAN.

The Empress

"You philosophers are lucky men. You write on paper & paper is patient. Unfortunate Empress that I am, I write on the susceptible skins of living beings."
- Catherine the Great

The Empress represents fertility, abundance, luxury & creativity. These things are interesting because you go through life perceiving the world as an individual, but it is also very clear that you can't play this game solo. As a non-conformist artist, the conflict between the individual & the group is especially pronounced to me. Life was a constant struggle to assert the value of my individuation growing up. However, I knew that I was incomplete as a human as soon as I hit puberty. Luckily for me, I found my Empress in Katie, who completed my creative circle! These things can feel particularly futile growing up, especially if you're as impatient as I was! Growing up, It's difficult if not impossible to know if things are going to turn out alright, so I felt a certain kind of extreme pressure, which I think is just natural. Anyhow, I was very lucky in finding Katie, someone who matches me, but also complements me in many ways. Besides the complementary male & female energies, one has to find similarly complementary energies in a partner. The Empress is a mother, a creator & nurturer. She can represent the creation of life, romance, art or business. The Empress can represent the germination of an idea before it is ready to be fully born & the need to be receptive to change. These are all things I need & our world needs. I put the Empress in front of where the ocean crashes on the shore, which is a fertile place & one of my favorite places. The cherubs on top of the throne are our three children.

SEFIN

The Chariot

"The demons are innumerable, appear at the most inconvenient times & create panic & terror. But I have learnt that if I can master the negative forces & harness them to my chariot, then they can work to my advantage."
- Ingmar Bergman

The Chariot represents action, drive & confident decision. Sometimes you just need to ignore the other options & go forwards with energy & drive. Like the horses (or pigs, in this case), you might have to mask or suppress things that are spooking you. Like the charioteer you have to hold on, stay the course & be bold. I tried to capture some Motörhead level energy with the piece. I thought of Thor with his chariot being driven by the goats Tanngrisnir & Tanngnjóstr. Because of this the charioteer is a sort of generic Northern mythic character. The Chariot & the charioteer are one, neither is that important by itself. The castles in the background represent accumulated wealth that the Chariot has launched from. The Charioteer is controlling the direction of the chariot with his mind & the moon faces in his armor symbolize his mighty subconsciousness. The spear he carries is the Spear of Destiny, the same spear that supposedly pierced the side of Christ, was possessed by King Herod & Hitler, inspired Napoleon, made an appearance in Wagner's Parsifal & which imbues the holder with incredible powers. I am a firm believer that fortune favors the bold, but I also recognize that constantly charging forwards is not sustainable. You've got to stop & rest. I spent almost an entire decade charging forward like the Charioteer & it took a stroke to slow me down. My inclination is still to charge forward!

VII

Strength

"Strength does not come from winning. Your struggles develop your strengths. When you go through hardships & decide not to surrender, that is strength."
- Arnold Schwarzenegger

Strength is necessary for most things in life. This image doesn't represent muscular, physical strength but mental strength. The image shows a woman who has tamed a dragon of destruction & chaos, mastered it. The woman uses her gentleness to calm the beast who she then has dominion over to use as she pleases. The beast sits on a pile of bones of things it has destroyed. She is looking out over a maze representing a long, complicated journey & a mountain representing a far-off destination, the Tower is there to give perspective. When I was a kid I wanted to be strong like the Hulk or Popeye, I did get quite strong! Stronger than anyone else I knew. What I didn't know was that this interior strength was a goal or something to be admired until much later in life. I began to notice & value interior strength when I was a teenager. This quiet, non-showy strength is a value that wasn't on display for me as a child, but I have come to really value. You didn't encounter it often in the 1980s. If you take on a higher level of consciousness you come to view adversaries as learning opportunities instead of obstacles to overcome, not something to require brute strength over. Some obstacles do require brute strength to overcome, but these should be viewed like a job you need a tool for.

SEAN
2017

Wheel of Fortune

"His success may be great, but be it ever so great the wheel of fortune may turn again & bring him down into the dust."

- Gautama Buddha

The Wheel of Fortune is cool because it traditionally shows both the upright & reversed meanings of the card in the art. The Wheel of Fortune says, "What goes up must come down & then up again." The upright positioning of the card symbolizes good luck, cycles, destiny & a turning point. The Wheel of Fortune is shown here as a windmill being powered by the invisible but mighty wind. The windmill itself is in a valley with cemetarial grounds & is manned by a mysterious, shrouded character. The barrel next to the door symbolizes wealth but also mystery, "What's in the barrel?" The Hebrew letters Yod, Heh, Vav & Heh are on each sail with a corresponding creature. The letters spell out the unpronounceable name of God. I view God as the Universal Will, not any kind of anthropomorphized understanding. God requires no human acknowledgment, our striving is enough. The idea of the art is that the wheel is God. The windmill is essentially a deliverer of civilization to humanity in a way few recognize. The creatures are the Holy King representing the highest of human achievement, the Monkey representing our basic biological drives, the Monster representing the distortions that pervert our fundamental goodness & Death which ends it all. A hoop snake (symbol of the cyclical infinite, the infinite is easier to deal with mentally if you view it as cyclical) rolls down the road to remind viewers of the cosmic play going on.

SEAN

The Hanged Man

"An easy way for the blind to go, A clever path for the fools who know,
The secret of the Hanged Man, the smile on his lips."

- Iron Maiden

The Hanged Man symbolizes independence from the flock, pause, surrender, letting go, new perspectives & an inability to do for self. You're going to have a lot of time & see a new perspective hanging like this! I used to do things like this to myself all the time, growing up. It's just a great way to be able to see the world differently. I was thinking of Odin & Christ when coming up with this drawing. I drew the figure as a Rocker in the mode of Roger Daltrey & Robert Plant, who evoke Odin & Christ in their own ways. To me, a Rocker is a person who puts them in these situations as a way of life & needs all sorts of people's help to prop him up, even moreso with the addition of addiction. I come from this, am sympathetic with & understand this type. I was raised in & fought against this milieu to establish myself & survive. I am under no delusion that no one should need the help of others, I just fought against the culture of dependency. The Hanged Man's legs are bent into the shape of the number four. The man has coins falling from his pockets, which symbolizes the way these characters tend to have an "easy come, easy go" attitude towards money. Despite the obvious flaws of this character, he is enlightened & this is symbolized by his halo. Because of his predicament, he has a lot of time to think, so his thoughts are deep. He might not have the ability to think himself out of this position but his thoughts are worthy of respect.

SEAN
XII

Death

"It is as natural to die as to be born." - Francis Bacon

I used to be very afraid of death, i'd get a chill in my stomach & butterflies just thinking about it. As I've gotten older & lived through the death of my mother & even died myself, I'm just not afraid of death anymore. I'm open to the feelings of loss & grief that come with death but I don't fear them & I don't think you should fear them either. I think a healthy desire to live & a love of life is necessary as a human & for society, but death is a healthy part of life too. The Death card isn't necessarily bad, it represents an end to things but also an inevitable beginning of something new or even a making way for the new. I didn't feel like these tendencies were that strong in me, but since experiencing death, their presence at all feels very strong & profound to me. I feel like a new person or that I'm experiencing a new life. In a way, fearing death is like fearing the change in seasons, or fearing change in general. This fear is terribly unhealthy & probably says something profound about the wrongness of our culture. Either way it's inevitable so the fear isn't serving you in any function. The art shows a skeletal warrior marching through fields of bones, marked with some headstones & a Mausoleum. In the distance there are two towers symbolizing strongholds of destiny. In the distance the sun rises symbolizing a new day.

XIII
SEAN·2017

The Devil

"The Devil pulls the strings which make us dance; We find delight in the most loathsome things. Some furtherance of Hell each new day brings, & yet we feel no horror in that rank advance."
- Charles Baudelaire

I have a funny relationship with the Devil. Most of the subcultures I've been involved with have been very friendly to the Devil & anti-Christianity. I was a Satanist for a few years (to shake off years of Leftist moralism) & I am still quite fond of Anton LaVey. I like the Devil as a monster & as an antagonist to the anthropomorphized vision of God, but I have found myself so removed from that sphere of thinking that it doesn't ring true to me. I have tried to play the role of the Devil for the morally sanctimonius in the past, but I really feel like it's not my fight & I feel that humanity's propensity towards the negative or selfishness doesn't need any encouragement at this point. I still am not trustful of moralism at all. So, I feel that elementally the Devil is still very useful, but not necessarily useful as something I need to embody. The card symbolizes the shadow self, attachment, addiction, restriction & sexuality. The art shows the Devil in the mode of Medieval portrayals hoisting a woman & man by chains. These people are shackled by their Earthly desires. The woman is ruled by the Moon above her & the man is ruled by Saturn above him. The Devil is shown as the ruler of the Earth, which balances on an Illuminati pyramid, taking advantage of people's lesser instincts. The whole thing is taking place on a theatrical stage to show how unreal it all is.

The Tower

"It's like in the great stories.... Full of darkness & danger they were. & sometimes you didn't want to know the end, because how could the end be happy? How could the world go back to the way it was when so much bad had happened? But in the end, it's only a passing thing, this shadow. Even darkness must pass."
- Sam Gamgee as written by JRR Tolkien

The Tower has strong relevance for me, it has come to represent having a stroke. The card can mean life-changing upheaval, chaos, revelation & awakening. I remember lying in the hospital bed thinking, "This sort of thing doesn't happen to me." But it did. Going into drawing this I wanted to evoke the Bad Brains self titled album & 9-11. While I was drawing these cards, I came to realize that so many of the big events since the millenium had correlative Tarot cards, but the country wasn't learning any of the lessons that the cards can teach. The moral of the card is like the Flight of Icarus (In Greek mythology, Icarus was the son of the master craftsman Daedalus, the creator of the Labyrinth. Icarus & Daedalus attempt to escape from Crete by means of wings that Daedalus constructed from feathers & wax. Daedalus warns Icarus first of complacency & then of hubris, instructing him to fly neither too low nor too high, lest the sea's dampness clog his wings or the sun's heat melt them. Icarus ignores Daedalus's instructions not to fly too close to the sun, causing the wax in his wings to melt. He tumbles out of the sky, falls into the sea & drowns.) mixed with the Tower of Babel (A Biblical myth, a united human race in the generations following the Great Flood, speaking a single language & migrating eastward, comes to the land of Shinar. There they agree to build a city & a tower tall enough to reach heaven. God, observing their city, tower & hubris, confounds their speech so that they can no longer understand each other & scatters them around the world.). In the art people leap out of the Tower in terror accepting this terrible change, but not wanting to face it. The figures are the same as in the Devil card. The lightning has struck down the Tower we have built up formerly giving us the rare opportunity to rebuild in a new way, do it all the same or cry in the rubble & give up. While having the stroke totally up-ended our world & I wouldn't wish one on anyone, the lessons learned from it couldn't be learned in any other way.

XVI
SEAN

The Moon

"The moon is friend for the lonesome to talk to."

- Carl Sandburg

When I was a young Punk I was a lunatic. I was a lunatic in the traditional sense of being crazy (probably still am) but also in the sense that I was a Moon fanatic. I can remember being as drunk as possible & just looking to the Moon for guidance, for something, multiple times. I am drawn to the moon. I have two moon tattoos. While the Moon is traditionally associated with feminine or yin energy, I have always portrayed the Moon as the Man in the Moon, but he is a weird man. The card can mean intuition, illusion, dreams, vagueness, instability, deception, anxiety, fear, misconception, the subconscious & insecurity. In the art, the Moon itself is shooting down some energy to the Earth, which it doesn't have dominion over, but it does have some power over. The towers represent the borders of the known, they have windows in the shapes of alchemical symbols. The whole thing is taking place near the ocean, a place of profound mystery & possibility that the Moon rules over. On the right is a dog barking at the moon & on the left is a Weird, carrying a barrel of moonshine. In the water are twelve fish, one for each month of the year. The Moon is flanked by a pair of giant moths, insects of the night & mystery.

SEAN

The Sun

If I had to choose a religion, the sun as the universal giver of life would be my god.
- Napoleon Bonaparte

As a redhead, I grew up avoiding the Sun, tending to some horrible sunburns with lots of lotion & having the looming threat of skin cancer always on the horizon. I couldn't be out in the sun longer than fifteen minutes without sunscreen. Since moving to Oregon from California, the Sun has increased in importance with the exponential decrease in sunburns. I now love the Sun & see it as a personal symbol. My first word as a baby was "Light", which I take as a personal mission of illumination. The card can mean positivity, optimism & freedom, things that I came to really believe in as I embraced the Sun. In my art, the Sun is missing its left eye, which means "See No Evil" in my cosmology. The Sun lights up the whole sky. The Sun delivers six drops of fertile power to the Earth acknowleging that all earthly power is granted by the sun. The fortress is a distinct man-made attempt at control which is made small & irrelevant by the grandeur of the Sun. Before the wall are a couple of lowly soldiers milling about to reinforce the smallness of man in comparison with the sun. Flowers spring up in the ruins of older, forgotten attempts at permanence again showing the overpowering strength of the Sun.

SEAN·17
19

The Minor Arcana

"Remember that the Tarot is a great & sacred arcanum - its abuse is an obscenity in the inner & a folly in the outer. " - Jack Parsons

The Minor Arcana pertains to more ordinary, human-level things, not the large, symbolic imagery of the Major Arcana. I based my interpretations loosely on the 1910 Rider-Waite deck, which was one of the first decks to treat these cards less like the ordinary playing card suits & actually attempt to illustrate what these cards mean. I started out relating less to the Minor Arcana, but the more I got into the Tarot, the more I thought the Minor Arcana fascinating. Each suit has a number of different names & each face relates to different energies & pertains to an ordinary set of playing cards. The numbers in the suits all mean different things like the threes mean creativity, growth & completion & the sevens mean reflection, assessment & knowledge. All the numbers have an assigned meaning which I attempted to capture with each card's illustration.

Wands

"It is with our passions as it is with fire & water, they are good servants, but bad masters."
- Aesop

The suit of Wands corresponds with the Clubs hand in ordinary playing cards. Clubs are connected with the element Fire, the will, masculine energy, fertility, creativity, originality & ambition. I like the to represent Wands as clubs, wands or rods. I also thought about the nature of mixing this fiery element with wooden wands or clubs & how that fiery energy can destroy that very vehicle that embodies it. Sort of going with the "Burning bridges" aphorism. Also, I feel like I've burned my candle at both ends since I was 18 or so & only stopped when I had the stroke. I like clubs in general, because I feel like there is a certain kind of person in this world that needs a good clubbing & never seems to get it. In my first attempt at the Tarot, I interpreted the Wands as sausages, & I probably would have gotten more into representing them as such.

SEAN

SEAN

SEAN

SEAN

Cups

"Love is the crowning grace of humanity, the holiest right of the soul, the golden link which binds us to duty & truth, the redeeming principle that chiefly reconciles the heart to life, and is prophetic of eternal good." -Petrarch

The suit of Cups or Chalices corresponds with the Hearts hand in ordinary playing cards. Cups are connected with the element Water & emotions. With the Cups suit I viewed this watery world which had elements of English seaside resorts & embodied by my favorite West Coast seaside towns. I wanted to represent the Cups with barrels, steins & goblets! As I got into the suit I realized that I was the King of Cups. Now that I've had ego death & actual death, this seems less plausible or important to me, but for who I was when I was doing these cards I definitely FELT like the King of Cups. Now, I've got this light switch emotional response to stimulus from the stroke, which is cool for finding stuff funny or makes controlling angry responses even easier, but it also means I cry very easily, which is great for emotional openness but can be more disruptive than I'd like. Anyhow, it's good to get in touch with your emotions, even as a relatively liberated & iconoclastic man, I'm still awash in the gender culture of the USA & there are norms about emotional repression that are there regardless of how much I'm conscious of their being. I've always been a heart on my sleeve kind of guy, I don't really have an option, but it makes it difficult to navigate the vast majority of people who wear a collectively agreed upon heart on their sleeves.

SEAN

SEAN.

SEAN

SEAN

SEAN

SEAN
7.

Coins

"Poverty makes you sad as well as wise." - Bertolt Brecht

The suit of Coins corresponds with the Diamonds hand in ordinary playing cards. Coins are connected with the classical element of Earth, the physical body & wealth. With the Coins suit I was going with a fairly standard interpretation & didn't get too far with my own thought & world as to the cards. It's mostly just because Katie didn't draw too many of the coins cards for me to work on! I did come up with the castle as a symbol of wealth, which repeats throughout the Tarot Goblinko but didn't make its way into the Coins just because I didn't draw enough of them. I've heard people speaking negatively about wealth since I was a kid, growing up in a left-leaning city, but I think the healthiest attitude you can have about money is that it is a tool, which isn't useful unless you use it. So I think hoarding or showing off wealth is a problem, but having money in itself is not a problem. Think about money elementally, it should flow & be level. Imbalance causes problems anywhere, & wealth imbalance has never been higher. In Oakland, where I grew up, there was a lot of wealth inequality which tainted everything, this was amplified if you compared Oakland to neighboring cities. If you think about money like water, you can over-water plants, stagnant water causes rot & disease, dried up plants whither & die & ultimately water seeks its own level.

SEAN

SEAN

Swords

"Don't leave home without your sword - your intellect." - Alan Moore

The suit of Swords corresponds with the Spades hand in ordinary playing cards. Swords are connected with the element Air, the intellect & the word. The other edge of the Sword is that it can herald misfortune & represent power without direction. I dig the Tarot/Alchemical way of thinking because it acknowledges that the elements are incomplete & need each other to balance things out. I think it's very important to view everything as incomplete & needing the assistance of the other to make things work. For Swords I was content to using the obvious visual choice, but I also wanted to reference Motörhead because of "The Ace of Spades".

When I drew the Ten of Swords I actually felt like I was on top of the world. I had really hit my stride in terms of just being able to create what I wanted to & be able to communicate it to my audience in a way that that I had never been able to, also to be able to float the family on the money I was pulling in. The Ten of Swords means "Rock Bottom" & while I haven't felt that way for more than a few minutes since having the stroke, I've definitely lost a lot since then, this is just a fact. Anyhow, the card means a feeling of hopelessness, the darkness before the dawn, feeling like a victim or a martyr or just bottoming out in general. Again, this is not a kind of feeling that I think I'm even capable of at this time, but I've felt this way in my youth & sympathize with people who are feeling this way. I used this card for what turned out to be the final issue of PORK magazine but again, this wasn't intentional at all but it was thematically appropriate as it was soon followed by my mom dying & then the stroke.

SEAN

SEAN

SEAN

SEAN

Tarot Goblinko
by Sean Äaberg
Back the Kickstarter! April 13th-May 13th
LIVE ON KICKSTARTER NOW!

by Sean Äaberg
LIVE ON KICKSTARTER

Process

"The artist must train not only his eye but also his soul." - Wassily Kandinsky

Before I gained success as an artist I was an art teacher for children. I learned so much as a teacher about how to be an artist that it shouldn't be overlooked. Trying to communicate with kids how to do art day after day really got me to focus on what I was trying to do as an artist & to understand art as a communications medium. Part of what I was trying to do was use readily available art tools to make the work. Because of this I drew on cheap card stock using cheap mechanical pencils & Sharpies, the most expensive art supply I used was Mars Plastic erasers (something similar to these is now available at the grocery store). My teaching intention here was that art supplies should not be precious & you should be able to execute high-quality work with what was on hand. While I initially watercolored pictures, I eventually used photoshop to emulate the mechanical coloring you'd find in old comic books & the like, this was specifically to get good reproduction of the colors for print which was my chosen means of expression. For the Tarot Goblinko I bought & read as many books on the tarot as I could find. Katie would draw a hand of cards to do & I would research each of those cards before interpreting it. The only cards I chose to draw out of this order were Death & the Sun which I drew as PORK covers & Strength which I drew for a custom jacket that Katie was working on.

For each of the cards I'd do my research in our library & then do some thinking on the subject. When I did the pencils I did them super fast & loose, doing them as quick as possible to get the ideas & general geometry down. If there was something I needed a reference for (like the mescaline cacti) I'd look up references for that later & just draw a placeholder shape in the meantime. This allowed the initial framework of the piece to be as pure as possible, especially when the final inks were going to be so laborious & tight, with no room for loosey goosey expression! For pencils I prefer to use a soft lead & a soft touch so that I don't have to do any hard erasing & the pencil doesn't leave impressions on the paper.

For the inks I do a first run over the whole thing with a regular sized Sharpie. This makes any decisions final because I also never use white out! I have to make sure any details I wasn't sure on were correct & do any final image research I might have put off.

For the colors I decide on a couple of contrasting central colors & then a third color if the piece needs one for clarity. I then break each color into two or three tones. I break the piece into rough color blocks first & make sure the colors are working well & change them if I need to. I then start tightening up the colors & adding details. I have a bold, limited color palette inspired by old comics & blacklight posters. I chose to use this palette partially because the trend towards muted tones is totally boring to me.

SEAN

I tend to not think much about my compositions, if I do, it's very quick & draws from my extensive & intuitive knowledge of sacred geometry, numerology & graphic design. It's important to know the purpose of the piece. Tarot Cards are supposed to be iconic, so that's what I went for. If there are reference points I make sure I know how they look or I research & sketch them out later.

After I do the first pass over the piece, I go over it again with an ordinary Sharpie & thicken lines if need be & fill in black spaces. This is the time I add shadows & the like. Sometimes the blacks just want to take up more space & they let me know!

For the colors on this one I wanted to do a contrasting red & green "Christmas" scheme. I use this scheme frequently & I got it from a Roger Dean Rolling Stones tour book he put together in 1978. I like the way the reds shine out of the greens.

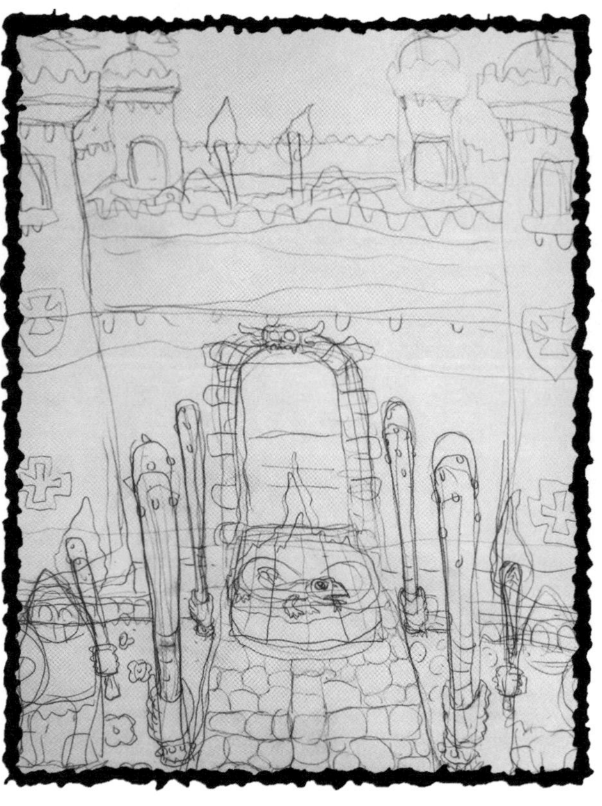

For the final stage of drawing I do the stippling & shading with a thinner pen. I would usually do this with the fine tip Sharpie, but I'd use other pens as well. This is a very laborious period & it takes me the most time. This period is also the time when I get to meditate on the piece & really think about the other drawings I'm going to do in the future.

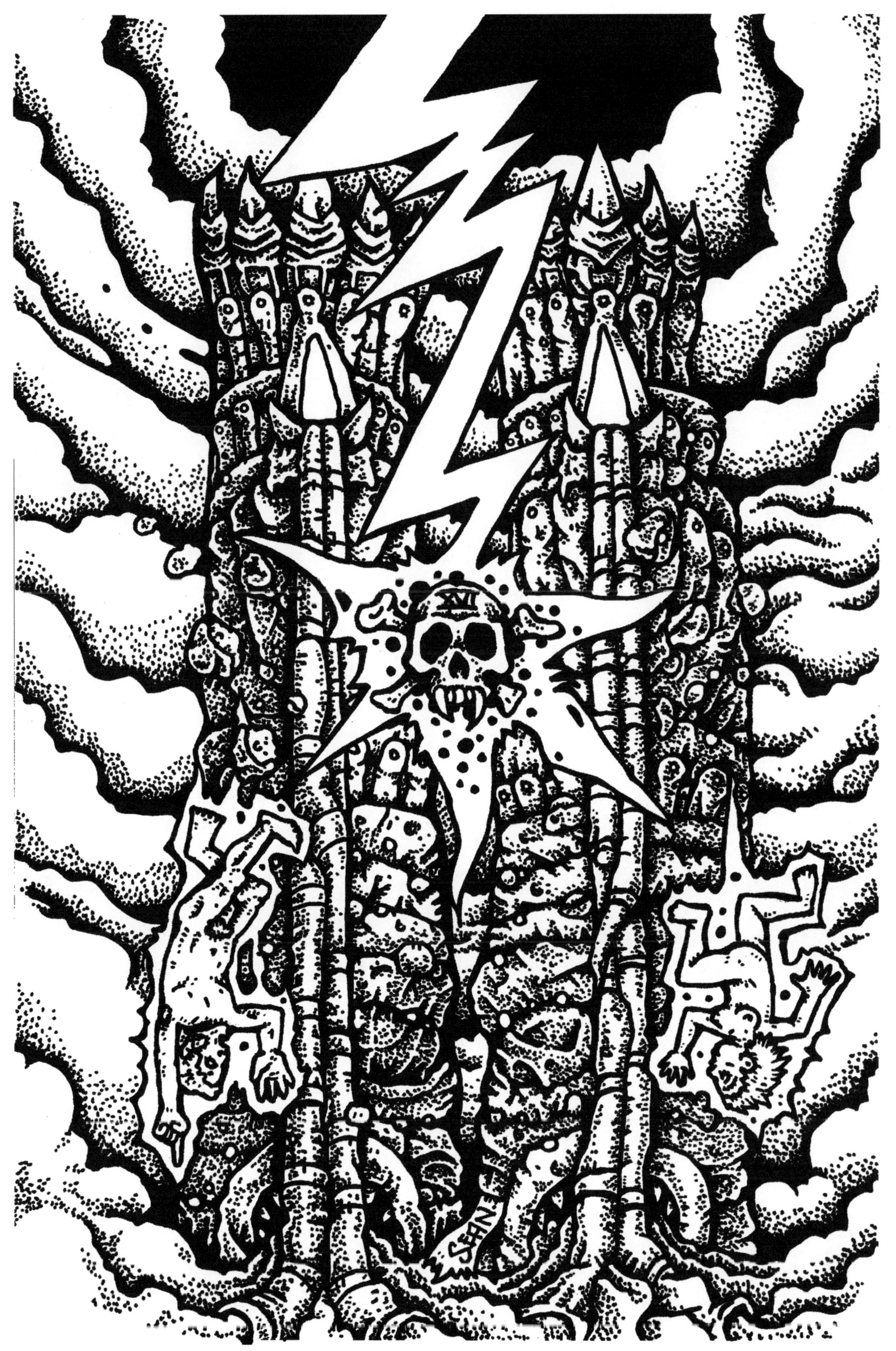
XVII
SEAN

My wife Katie does a variety of textile arts & applique with embroidery is one of them. She made this vest in 2018 for our friend Anne. I originally did the Strength card for the vest, but I decided to finish it & use it as the cover of PORK 26 as well. The initial stages of my drawings are simple enough to replicate with a sewing machine if you're good, so Katie used the piece before I added all the details & rendered it. I think it turned out great!

SEAN
2017

In Conclusion

"The Tarot embodies symbolical presentations of universal ideas, behind which lie all the implicits of the human mind, & it is in this sense that they contain secret doctrine, which is the realization by the few of truths embedded in the consciousness of all."

- A.E. Waite

I love universals. I love old systems of things that are firmly established & people understand or can come to understand. Because of this, the Tarot means a lot to me in terms of art. I honestly don't care much about or believe in divination, but there are some very talented Tarot readers out there. I just don't believe in or need divination. I had every intention of completing the Tarot Goblinko but life threw me for a loop. I had enough good intention & will power to pave the Road to Hell twice over! As we say around here, "having a stroke completely sucks but..." We're such an optimistic/silver-lining people there are a lot of life lessons that we learned by going through this catastrophe. That's the lesson, no one would choose to have such a life-changing event occur, but what's important is what you do with that event & your relationship to it. It's like a lot of the events that have been happening globally. We can play the "poor me" card, but that's a bad play. It stinks to live in "Interesting Times" but we are all being tried, we all have the choice to come out of this as better people, if we survive! The whole world has the chance to be reborn in this trauma. While I & no one can be sure what the future holds for any of us, if we're going to be blind sided by yet another tragedy or what, I do know that we can roll with whatever cards we're dealt.

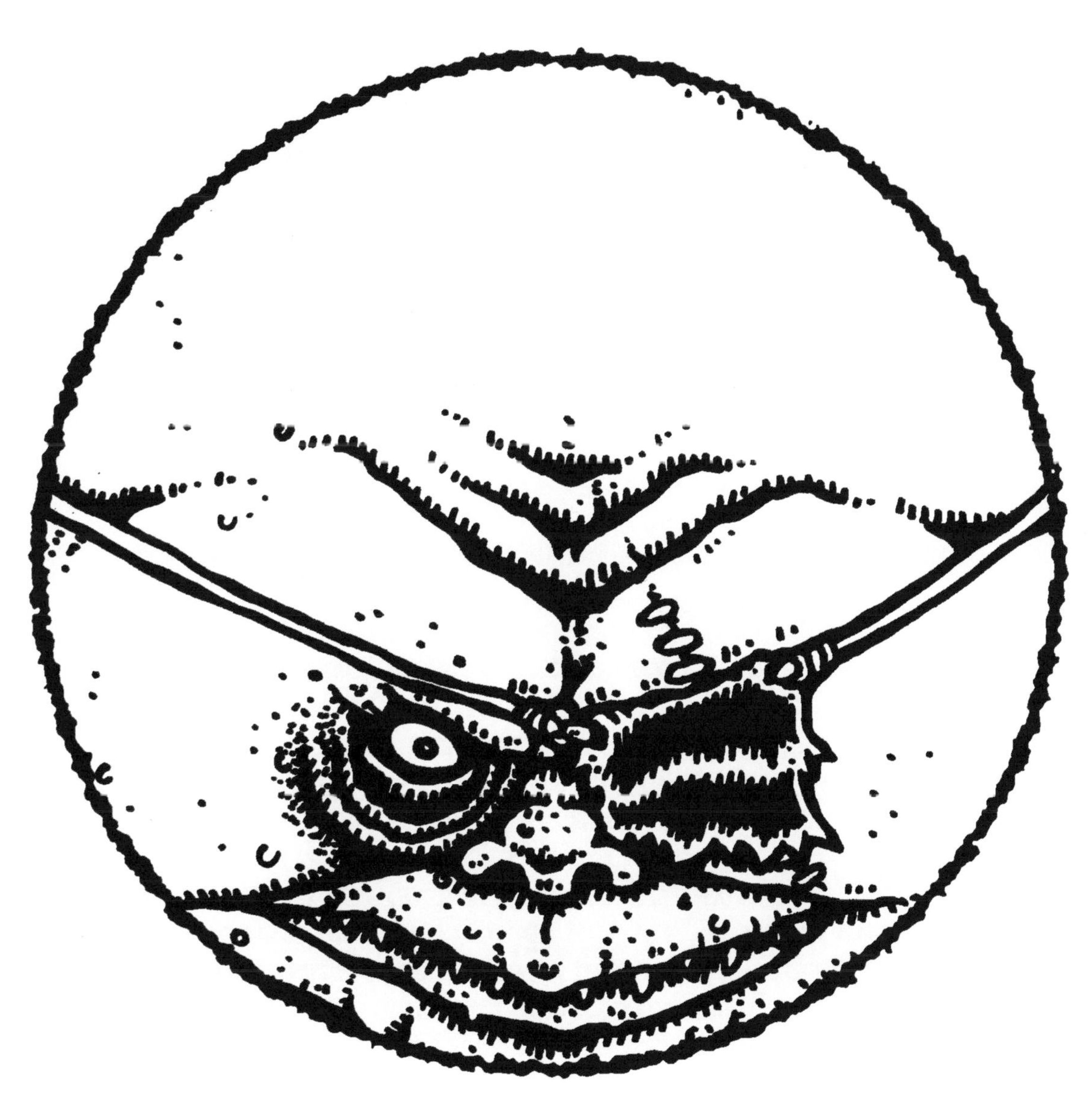

Sean Äaberg was born & raised in Oakland, California into a bohemian family. In 1988 at age twelve he discovered zines, the Church of the Subgenius & Punk all at the same time which gave his world of Garbage Pail Kids, Pee-Wee's Playhouse, Dr. Demento & MAD Magazine direction & drive. Sean has viewed his visual art as part of a series of cultural systems & tries to incorporate all levels of culture with his work. In 2000, Sean married fellow East Bay artist Katie Krause (now Aaberg), & they started **GOBLINKO** after his Punk name "Goblin" as an umbrella for their projects. In 2011 Sean decided to give big zines a go again & **PORK** Magazine was born. **PORK** covered Rock&Roll, Weirdo Art & Bad Ideas, going for an inclusive, big-tent approach instead of targeting little niche groups. **PORK** influenced a couple generations of lowbrow artists, Rock bands & entrepreneurs who copied the **GOBLINKO** business model. As the internet & smart phones in particular changed the way people consume media, Äaberg decided that making games would better fit where he & his audience were at. **DUNGEON DEGENERATES** was released in 2017. **PORK** ceased publication of May, 2018. In September, 2018 Äaberg suffered a severe stroke & is now recovering & figuring out what to do next. Sean lives in Portland, Oregon with his wife Katie & their three kids.

Sean Äaberg photo by Katie Aaberg